Angels and Daffodils

DIANE EVERETT

Copyright © 2022 by Diane Everett
Cover Design © 2022 by Evelyn Rainey

All rights reserved. No part of this book may be reproduced, scanned, or distributed in any printed, audio or electronic form without permission. Such piracy of copyrighted materials is a violation of the author's rights and is punishable by law.

ISBN-13: 978-1-946469-23-6

ShelteringTree.Earth, LLC Publishing
PO Box 973, Eagle Lake, FL 33839

ShelteringTreeMedia.com

DEDICATION

Angels and Daffodils is dedicated to my family.
If no one has told you yet today that they love you,
let me be the first person to say,
"I love you."

CONTENTS

Foreword	i
Priceless	1
A New Day	3
By Its Very Nature	5
Upon Rising	7
Certain Value	8
Walking Into Tomorrow	9
We Have God	10
Embrace of Freedom	11
We Witnessed the Changes	13
When the Wind Blows	14
In the Woods	16
When the Wind Has Sailed	17
Like You	18
Drums That Call	20
Home At Last	21
The Healing That Comes	22
Homeward Bound	24
Restoration	26
Attachment	27
James Whitcomb Riley – Poet	29
Your Image	31
Endangered Lives	33

Reborn	34
Today Different	35
It Seems	36
Addiction	37
I, the Mighty	38
A Love for His Children	39
Ageless Sages Gathered	40
He Came for You	42
Misstep	43
Angels Will Keep	45
Nurturing	46
No Shadows	47
Pain's Delight	48
Reaching	49
Recovering God	51
A Glimpse of Who We Are	52
At This Day's End	53
Step by Step	54
Blooms From Underneath	56
Flower Fields	57
Fly Me High	58
For Leon Matheny	59
Golden Jewel	60
Growth	61
Hold Me for a Moment	62

Gray Clay	63
The Door	66
If You Never Changed a Thing	68
Upon Awakening	69
Innocence Believes	70
We Admitted	71
Golden Package	72
Without My God	74
Passing	75
The Wound	76
And I Cried	78
Too Many Times	80
Fertile Soil	81
Play to Win	82
To Choose Again	84
Memories of You	85
Precious Memories	86
About the Poet	87
Discussion Guide	88

FOREWORD

When Diane first walked into my *Writers at Unity* group, she looked terrified but excited too, much as a child would look while staring at a lion on safari for the first time. She carried with her a rag-tag notebook filled with what I came to realize were treasures. It took a while. She had her friend Donna read her poems outloud the first few meetings. Then, assured of our love and acceptance, she began reading them aloud herself.

The poems were about a wounded life, filled with sorrow and horror, betrayal and disloyalty (her own as well as others'). The weakness of her mortality, however, was tempered with her undeniable sense of eternity, hope, joy, grace, and love – of God, of humanity, of the unbounded universe, and of herself.

It took a while before I could convince her to publish her poems – years, I believe, but her first book **Rise Dove Awakened** outsold the entire list of *Sheltering Tree Publishing's* books the first month and continues to do well. This book, **Angels and Daffodils**, will break your heart and heal it. When I read the first poem she presented, I had to stop and walk around the house and find my center, because, as you know, none of us are strangers to despair. But as you read this collection of poems, you will come to realize that none of us are strangers to hope, or joy, or love, either. That's what Diane offers here -

Evelyn Rainey ~ American Educator, Author, & Publisher

PRICELESS

Angels and Daffodils

Dreams that come true

A life that's worth living

Designed just for you

Already paid for

All the treasures in store

Now you're given a new key

To unlock every door

This true understanding

Is yours to employ

As you walk down the hallway

New freedom, new joy

Angels and Daffodils

Dreams that come true

Freedom to love

All that is given to you

A new vision to live in

New sights to behold

A life full of treasures

More precious that gold

These are yours for the asking

Such grace without measure

Love is the key

Your own life is the treasure

A NEW DAY

To start today

With compassion

Kindness to self

Moving and being active

Household chores

Preparing for today's journey

Compassion for a co-worker

Forgiveness given

Slights avoided

Attentiveness

I hear you

I see you

You are safe

You are loved

You are valued

For your contribution

The energy you give

The light you bring

To the darkness

We will walk together

We are not alone

To start today with understanding

That this space I hold

Is not isolated or partitioned

We start the day with compassion

Today a new day

The same differently

BY ITS VERY NATURE

You fret for yesterday

The past

By its very nature

Is gone

You left it no choice

When you left it behind

You moved into today

You moved on

So here you are

With undone projects

Unresolved issues

Unhealed wounds

Startling, isn't it?

No more past

Nope, no future yet

It is not yet

And will

By its very nature of not being

Bring you no comfort

With what are you left

To live in

To be in

To have

Right here

Right now

By the very nature of its being

You are all the present has

To love

Be loved by

Be loved in

Enjoy this moment

It is designed just for you

And after all

By its very nature

It is all that there is

UPON RISING

As I wake and sit in quietness
The start of this new day
And ask You to receive me
In a quiet musing way
Then You unfold a mystery
That has puzzled me for years
And wipe away the doubt
That is like soft rain in tears
The world seems to unfold again
With sunbeams shining through
And You show me what You've chosen
For this child of Yours to do
That peace I find in seeking
Seems to please both You and me
And my trust improves with knowing
That I live in harmony
With the God of all Creation
As Your thoughts direct my own
And I abandon all my power
To the God I've always known

CERTAIN VALUE

Clasping certainty

The comfort of tightening life's grasp

To a distant appendage

Without a need to reason or evaluate

Pressing against the one

Who towers above

Precious

Simple

Compassion

An extension of need

An expression of love and trust

Having a meaningful value

As a child clinging to a mother's leg

WALKING INTO TOMORROW

The sun's warm rays

The wind's cooling

The expressed pain

The gentleness of a friend

The tears of surrender

The acknowledgement of defeat

The will to live

The presence of Love

The knowledge of God

The song of the birds

My feet

The hope of tomorrow based on today

I am grateful I have you

Please don't go away

WE HAVE GOD

Although we do not have each other
For our eyes to see
We know that we have God
Who lives eternally
To this truth we hold on rightly
For this peace will get us through
All the labors and the tasks
That we are asked to do
When the burden seems too heavy
We bring back to memory
All the promises Life gave us
Guaranteed through Calvary
That sweet Spirit full of Grace
Lives in you and lives in me
And in a world with darkness
Through the Spirit's eyes we see
Forever now
We'll seek Love
You in your way, me in mine
For Love has for each a purpose
And the plan is One Divine

EMBRACE OF FREEDOM

I looked at you this morning
And I knew that you were love
Your calmness drew me closer to your side
A tenderness of warmth I felt
 A longing to belong
A stripping down of selfishness and pride
I opened up myself to you
And inner secrets shared
A need in life to do more than survive
The hope that you believed in me
The power I could feel
My readiness to grow and be alive
You recalled a time of quest
Within your own existence
A time of search for life
That was your own
I reached for a new freedom
New joy of understanding
True happiness
That I had not yet known
You cautioned that though painful
I should resist a struggle

In only letting go would I be freed

So I gave up my own need to know

And gave control away

Now God's grace works sufficiently for me

WE WITNESSED THE CHANGES

Yellow melted into running pools of amber
Met by the cool blue of the sky
Flashing green sparkles of energy
Released reflections of red heat
Rainbows glistened on the water
We sat simply quietly
Aware of our pale smallness
Feeling vulnerable unnoticed on the sand
Summer's sun had faded
Fall had arrived in timely fashion
Winter became the whiteness
To wash away in Spring
The dead debris unneeded by Earth
We sat blessedly content
As we witnessed the changes
Of the seasons

WHEN THE WIND BLOWS

Spirit moves

Lights brighten

The beginning has begun again

Challenged to survive

Dawning fully

Filling freely all that is

While wars rage

Conflicts lighten

The end Illuminates itself

Illusions end

Victories cease

Life lives

Freeing the power

To fulfill its destiny

From beginning to end

Myself a part of

Not the whole

Fragments of space

Of time

Of consciousness

Of life

When the wind blows

Spirit moves

IN THE WOODS

I imagine myself
In the world of the Deer
Velvet feet swiftly carrying
My weight of this winter
Fast I move between the space of the trees
In the spring I will remember
To return and eat their new leaves
Down to the river
Over the stump
Where last summer
During the big rain
The tree was heard falling
We did not make it back
To our shelter in time
To keep from getting wet
Our hearts leaping with excitement
As the sun returned to the sky
Lighting the way
Content in the day
In the life of a Deer

WHEN THE WIND HAS SAILED

When the wind has sailed many ships
And the clouds have covered many skies
Our tears will have filled many seas
We will return to a place
Where this journey began
Finding safe harbor
Unafraid and comforted in the knowledge
That we receive our hearts' desires
To enter with freshness a new phase
And rediscover a completeness
We sought in the salt of life

LIKE YOU

Make me like

You

Mold me to Your Will

Do it please

While I am waiting

Quietly and still

For it is not my nature

Although I am tempted

To turn and stray away

Hold me God

Before I run

And waste another day

The power that I count on

A power not from me

A power that enabled You

To die and set me free

A love so far surpassing

Any love I've ever known

A love You gave Your life for

A love that rules my own

This love the only love I see

A love that died to set me free

And dead and buried rose again
For all Eternity
A love I long to cling to
And do the best I can
Please change me God
To be like you
And love me
Just the way I am

DRUMS THAT CALL

Steadily moving within the stillness

Listening to the water

That roams through the hills

Sunbeams glistening off the ripples

Flowing over each rock

Gently washing the face of each life

Its moving current

Flowing past where I stand

I feel the beat of my heart

Rhythmically steadfast

Leaning into and responding to

The drums that call to me

To the prosperity

Of a continuous flow

The rhythm of my heart

HOME AT LAST

The voice said,
"You don't have to hide anymore
You are allowed to feel
The intensity of emotion
Required to begin the healing"
Proportionately in minutes
The anguish of years
Is digested
A truth of how I perceive myself
Reached
Then transmuted
Into an awareness of inner beauty
With unbounded wonder of
Sight
Smell
Breath
Insight no longer abandoned
At home with myself

THE HEALING THAT COMES

The healing that comes

From releasing

The fear

The anger

The sadness

The unloved parts of me

The parts that have not

Been given the chance

To remember enjoyment

Things are not as they appear

Judgement enters expecting a seat

That it has occupied in the past

One that it has been allowed to hold

That seat is now given

To one who stands in front of it

And simply asks intrusions to leave

Having lost the use of that seat

There is no longer room for its obstructions

Then let my words sound a joyous tone

Let the love held within them

Bring a smile and sparkle

Of new life

At the end of this day

Let my words reflect the gratitude

To a Presence that loves unconditionally

My weaknesses as well as my strengths

Then on this day I am healed

HOMEWARD BOUND

I will make it home

I will live

Way past tomorrow

Into the sky

My love light shines

Nothing there to not adore

Bring it home

All the past

Whatever it was

That got me here

Bring it all home

To me

Sit and tell me

Where you have been

And what you have seen

Yesterday is gone

Tomorrow is still

An unknown dream

I will gather my Love and Grace

Find my seat

In this moment and time

Precious and holy little ones

That are mine to love
And be loved in
Welcome home

RESTORATION

You are such a feeling of newness
You send such a vision of light
The peace I find in believing
Makes everything turn out so right
This newness excitement
 And wonder
This vision that shines pure and true
The love that has carried me this far
Is the reason I say, "Thank you"
And if in this moment of glory
And if in this moment of might
The hope of the messages promised
Offers freedom to fuel the delight
Then the peace that I feel in believing
The love that will carry me home
The hope of the messages promised
Have restored me to faith of my own

ATTACHMENT

I am not able

To get close to you

You remind me

Of too many things

From my past

That have hurt or scratched

Even though not deeply

At surface level

When cut I bleed

When I am able

To control the bleeding

Stop the progress of a wound

I realize that it does matter

And will heal

When I am able to remain calm

Finding peace in this moment

I realize

That most of my life

Has been a series of hurting and being hurt

Injuries that come from attempting *to be*

Instead of knowing that *I am*

A series of both painful and joyous healings

I stand on healed wounds

Only images now

With unflinching emotions attached

I let go

Of the attachment

And let you in

JAMES WHITCOMB RILEY - POET

I remember I was young and impressionable

When I first read a poem you wrote

You sounded as though I could hear you

The first line I heard of yours

The one I took inside of me

The last line in the poem

The line I accepted as Truth

Your words were talking about life

You never mentioned death

I had the impression

That you did not believe in that

Life you talked to me about

Life you wrote about

I read life

I heard life

I lived a life through what you wrote

You were a safe refuge

You were the reality of a friend

At times I felt I missed you

Then I remembered

The first line I heard

The one I believed as a truth

Life you taught me to say

When the pain of separation resurfaced:

"He is not dead - he is just away"

YOUR IMAGE

I need you with tears tonight

The passion for life feels overwhelming to me

I have been away for so long

I feel I can never catch up

Would you help me catch up?

Are you asking me to become again

Someone I don't know

A different part of myself

I need you with reflective purpose

To remind me of how very far

We have traveled

Your hand in mine leading

I need you with a sigh

I cherish the companion

Who has been with me from my beginning

The love you give is my life's blood

The peace you share with me

Is the serenity I have sought

In this lifetime

You have taught me to be

The creation called child

The ways I seek you

Father Mother Child God

Thank you for being

All You are to me

My love, companion, serenity, my purpose

Thank you for the kindness that you bless me with

As you restore

My soul to Your image

Your image to my soul

ENDANGERED LIVES

I watched you soar with me
Your Eagle wings slightly tilted left
"Dip to the Southwest," you called out
So we sailed down through air
My mind motionless
The thrill of my heart
Made the clouds part
"Teach me to spiral!" I cried
Eger to teach
And fly free from my demands
You turned sharply
One great wave of air
My wings were young
My memory is dimly haunted
By my last sight of you
The look of your yellow eyes intense
Before the moment when an earth child
Felt the victory of its first kill
And I had to fly alone

REBORN

Accepting shared completeness

A willing spirit

Held deeply within

A lovely experience

Often hard to express

The ways of giving love

Made strongly visible

In daily challenges

Directly given

To help man transcend

To the element of humanness

Following a light

Constant in the knowledge

Of an undying love

TODAY DIFFERENT

Like new air

Regrouped molecules

Assembled for one moment's function

Changed and yet still changing

A peaceful presence

Energetically aware of the freshness

Mine all mine

The joyful calls of childhood

Laugh and live for this

The first arrival of newness

A moment within itself

Today different

IT SEEMS

It seems a great reality

Where inner secret shares

With a voice that brings such harmony

To a life so filled with care

My God allows me freedom

To walk now in this world

I am not buckled down inside

In a fetal position curled

The joy I have in seeking

Is a living truth for me

I practice it in all my ways

In all the paths I see

ADDICTION

The intensity of addiction
The remorse of unfulfilled lives
Mount Everest has been conquered by so few
And they surrendered to her majesty
Life will cause the growth
Will bring about the change
Mine the sanity
The reality to stay
Right here right now
Willing to remain present through the lesson
And not abandon the classroom I have chosen
This the daily challenge for my Will
The ever evident need to live fully
And still not to forget
The insanity of addiction

I, THE MIGHTY

Cheer up, cheer up

Ye weary souls

Ye lowly dandelions

Today to capture fields in glow

Speak yellow to the sun

For by the time you're fully grown

Your race will soon be run

Then, when your petals' brighter hues

Have turned to misty grey

I, the mighty wind-like child

Will blow them swift away

A LOVE FOR HIS CHILDREN

Praise be to God for the servants who follow
Not knowing what task they'll be asked to perform
Perhaps in much need, cold hungry or tired
With the Glory of God in His Love they are warm
Praise be to God for His loving salvation
He sought us and taught us to follow Him home
He came here to teach us the lessons we needed
And then took our own death upon Himself alone
Praise be to God for the victory he offers
That life won't be lost although tossed by a storm
All who He calls who will humble to serve Him
To those He'll give all and will keep them from harm
Praise be to God, to the God of all glory
The Father who sent His own son here to die
To show us His mercy the love for His children
Praise be to God, to the God Most High

AGELESS SAGES GATHERED

Their faces partly covered
By beard hair soft and inviting
With ease skintight hands
Passed over their chins
Down to the end
Of the grayish brown growth
Time had given to them all
Deep set eyes sparkled
Like unmined went granite
Reflecting full lives
Still laughing
Throughout the encampment
The sages gathered
Sheltered by oak trees moss laden canopies
Lying on coneless pine needle piles
Resting over logs
That had fallen to become new soil
Authentic in purpose
They pondered truth
Unraveling riddled pages
Of unforgotten rhymes
They listened

For the exposition of wisdom
Evening was first noticed
By the smell of wood fire embers
The darkness of night made evident
As yellow fire sparks melted into amber
And were carried away by cooling air
Throughout the evening's gatherings
No new truth was laid bare
No new hidden light of mystery was offered
Even so
They stayed long into the night
Throughout the encampment
Smaller lights were seen glowing
As they passed pipes to those left searching
And took turns blowing smoke rings

HE CAME FOR YOU

This disease taking many forms
This passion for denial
For the art form of lies
For the pleasure of deception
Cunning as a serpent
Gently as a dove
It has not been removed
Changed and still changing
I am diseased by the hardening
Of my heart to the truth
I allowed this beast within me
Saved only by a mighty Creator
That gives life
That suffers not the loss of death
The One who is pure in heart
The One who speaks only truth
The One who sees only mercy
Who says to my disease,
"You are the reason
I have come here"

MISSTEP

I faulted today
On my way to the Zoo
I turned right and then left
Which directly
Affected the flow
I got in my way
As I continued to move
About what I thought
Was a truth I would know
Which directly
Affected the flow
Then I thought
What a joke
What a farce
What a ploy
There is so much
In this life to enjoy
So I learned how to march
With joy in each step
Placing my feet
Where my purpose is met
Which directly

Affected the flow

ANGELS WILL KEEP

Tiredness, Tiredness
Call out for sleep
Then gently call again
Angels will keep
All of my memories
Tuck them away
Rest now sweet little one
Tomorrow you'll play
And when the slumber
Falls gently upon you
And when the day
Has said its goodbyes
Then sleep will enter
And quiet the little one
Tenderly kissing
Its sleep-heavy eyes

NURTURING

Your life as I see
On a daily level
Will eventually be like mine
Tree branches grow
Reach new levels
Toward new heights they climb
To fear for them is futile
They were meant to grow
Their purpose and the reason
Was not for them to know
The peace I find in seeking
Is somewhat like a tree
Questions that dig deep inside
Bring life that flows through me

NO SHADOWS

Inside darkness

I see light

Bright and overflowing

Filling me completely

There is born

Within my presence

Full delight

Breath

Wonder

Joy

As my soul takes flight

In the light

Where there are no shadows

PAIN'S DELIGHT

Sparkle teardrops
Shine through me
Tears of Love this world will see
Borne to be what you will be
The beauty that surrenders me
And when the tears have dried away
The memories left will still display
All the years that held you tight
Until you ventured into light

REACHING

I will make a crack

In this hardened foundation

This mortal point holding my feet

To the ground

With my head and hair dangling

Around my upside-down face

And I am stuck here

I will reach

I will seek the advice of good council

My steps have placed me

In this position

And these words

Are the echoes of words

I have heard before

In the repetition of resentment

Authenticity is

After all

Under the ash trays

So let me reach again and again

This may be my highest point of achievement

I cannot know that without

Stepping out

And moving forward
And then
This right now
In this moment
Is my very best
I will accept it as my very best
Grateful that at one point in my life
I achieved my highest and best good
And then true to my nature
I breathed it into being
As I turned a corner
And reached out again

RECOVERING GOD

Accept me birth

I will be born

Through the energy you give

I will know life

I will share painful feelings

I will have joyous freedom

I will not be denied

My choice to live

In whatever form I take

In this humanness

I will breathe newness

I will breathe life

I will live

A GLIMPSE OF WHO WE ARE

Round and climbing

Hills roll out of valleys

Following parallel lines

Laced with amber

As yellow daffodils collect

The sun's spark

This you and I are

Reflections of moments

Glimpses of a natural presence

Moment to moment

Transforming

Swaying in our loftiness

Falling to replenish the earth

AT THIS DAY'S END

It's late now

My body is tired

Worn down

By today's wandering through this world

Before I close to rest

I hold a small white feather

Left in memory of a song

A song sung many years ago

Still not forgotten

The nurturing of a winged prayer

Carried by voices

A choir in the clouds

This my world

A captured moment's thrill

Free to glide on moist air and enjoy

The peaceful presence of a life lived fully

Wise to desire the nurturing of self

That calls me to stillness

As I surrender to the clouds of rest

STEP BY STEP

Bump Bump

Thump Thud

As on in life we go

Hitting different bottoms

Weaving to and fro

Bump again then crash and burn

As afflicted often do

Until the lessons learned

It's over when it's through

Regroup

Gather strength

Remorse

Then start again to run life's course

Until I find another pain

Then Thump and Bump

And crash again

And finally when all seems done

And there's no strength

With which to run

I have no victories to display

And there appears to be no way

To regroup and start again

Then I sit down

And being still
Admit defeat because I'm ill
From ashes deep there grows a hope
That with the truth brings power to cope
With one more lesson one more time
This power of God is Love Divine

BLOOMS FROM UNDERNEATH

Even more shy
Than the flighting butterfly
The Lilly of the Valley
Tucked beneath their leaves
Sheltered from heat and wind
Connected to the vines of life
That hold them in uniformity
Their petals are strong
The whiteness of their beauty is bright
Bells that bring the Angels to light
Ever so slightly moving in rhythm
An assembly for all
To admire believing
That life although hidden
Brings expressions of joy
I smile when I find them
Always dancing

FLOWER FIELDS

Blue butterflies

Lightly orange spotted wings

Flap flap they fly

Higher lower all around

Softly leveling on the ground

Flower fields

Green stemmed with yellow petals

Sweetly they wait

Larger smaller varied sizes

Joining earth to meet with sky

And hold the feeding butterfly

FLY ME HIGH

Run with me
Fly me high
Through the air
On my string
Guide me as I pass over
Houses trees and telephone wires
Lead me to an open meadow
Release me into the blue sky
Laugh with me
As I dip and dance
Upon the currents of life
Reflecting my fondest moment
Mastering my greatest dream
Conquering my illusion

FOR LEON MATHENY

The lessons that you helped me learn
More precious than I knew
I thank and praise the Lord my God
For precious souls like you
Although I did not understand
In detail every thought
Again I'm grateful for the way
The love of Christ was taught
I know that through Christ's love for you
I have been led to grow
And Jesus precious Jesus
Is the one I've come to know

GOLDEN JEWEL

You are a golden jewel

Radiantly you glow

Joy you give

Laced with grace and passion

For life you call

With the sweetest of heart tones

You are the quality you give

Held together with meaning and purpose

You are a golden jewel

Priceless in every facet

GROWTH

Raindrops held with the flow
Of gentler rains long ago
Newness freshly made to spring
Up then down and back again
Like the teardrops that bounce and fade
Into a spring that has been made
Where all can see and know the joy
The life that pain could not destroy
Teardrops raindrops always flowing
My world within a world is growing
Changes cause a different hue
As my rainbow springs
Into full view

HOLD ME FOR A MOMENT

Kiss the morning

From my eyes

As mine look on

To see life unfold

The energy must change

For the presence of color

On the kaleidoscope to change

Pattern moves are noted

Lined up in perfection

Breathing in and out

The rhythm is harmonized

And I am held for a moment

In its brilliance

GRAY CLAY

Show yourself

Get unstuck

Then when I can see you in my words

When I can feel you come out of your hiding place

I will keep you safe and loved

Compassionately sit with you

You do not have to be afraid

Safety is not found in the hiding places

To know your value

You must be in the light

You must be seen to be freed

Anything other than that

Would hold no value

And you have so much value

So come out

And have your day

Your say what is what

Or was

Or whatever

To stay in the shadows

Only you know you are missing

That is the saddest place

When you don't even hear yourself
Ask for help
Or a hug
Or anything that life must give
I was there for so long
It became normal to not
To just not
Not feel
Not cry
Not laugh
Not think
Not want
That might seem sad except
Soon the life stuff starts to flow
Slowly controlled
Emotional pain hurts
Give it time gently
Crying takes a lot of energy
Thinking is confusing
Because it is well known
That if I cannot see you
Then you cannot see me either
Or something like that
I want you to be free
To teach me where the boundaries are
Where life starts and ends

I acknowledge you
Place you in a chair
Across from me
Putting a face on you and saying
You cannot control me any more
Thank you for the lesson
Now learned
I will face you
Call you out by name
Heal because of your presence
Your part in making my character
A forward movement of growth
I will live freely
Autonomous by the burden
Of knowing there is a part of me
That does not know how beautiful it is
Until it is seen

THE DOOR

On the other side of the doorway
At the top of the golden stairs
Water flowing pure and free
Life's renewal we will find there
Beautiful now a valley view
From top of mountains whitened hue
We have done what we must do
To reach the blessing here
On the other side of the doorway
Wherever it may be
There is a heaven waiting
For all humanity
Some will travel quickly
While others wait and pray
And learn to teach the lessons
That were lost along the way
On the other side of the doorway
Through the gates that lead above
There waits for each perfection
Designed by the hands of Love
With lifetimes interwoven
With the grace of gentle care
There is a heaven waiting

At the top of life's golden stairs

IF YOU NEVER CHANGED A THING

If you never changed a thing

I absolutely

Love you

The qualities that you show me

Are your gifts

The presence of your life

Here

Now

I smile at that truth

Laugh with Joy

At your playfulness

Your Joy of life

Well lived and wiser

If you never changed a thing

I find peace in knowing

You remain in love

Centered on a firm foundation

Anchored by choice

To the gift of life

UPON AWAKENING

I found myself
I discovered I am myself
On this journey when I needed myself I was here
I may lose myself again and again
Only to find myself again in the end
Perhaps a little bit older and wiser
Realizing that I was never really lost

INNOCENCE BELIEVES

Tell me a story

With a pretty ending

With tiny blue flowers

And soft green grass

Tell me the morning truth

The one that gives the flowers

Their reason to live

Truth that comes

From being a part of creation

The kind of story

A child's innocence believes

Where fountains flow endlessly

Without beginning or end

Just because we want them to

Remind me of the forever

Where my memory lives

Please tell me a story

One that I will believe

Because you've been there

Please tell me a story

So that I will never forget

Where I belong

WE ADMITTED

The powerlessness that rests in you
Divinely given to see you through
That hides the deepest shadow's pain
Until it's time to see again
Until it's time to grow
Until it's time for love's return
Then sweet the power at fullest glow
Will gently enter evenly flow
And you will know what you will know
The powerlessness that rests in you

GOLDEN PACKAGE

I found a golden package

You had left behind unnoticed

And I questioned if

It had been left for me

The inscription on the card read

For the one who now is holding

For the one who now is pondering

In their hands this gift of life

I wanted to believe

That the package held a vision

More than anything I wanted

For the package to be real

The inscription on the card meant

This is a new beginning

The happiness and joy are yours

If you will just look inside

I took off all the paper

And I saved it for tomorrow

But that took too long to get here

So I opened it today

All the joy I found in looking

All the treasures that were waiting

It was full of little boxes
One designed for every day
In each box at new day's dawning
I found a special present
So I looked into the mystery
Of a life designed for me
And though every day was different
I no longer woke in sorrow
I looked forward and rejoiced in
The gifts of each new day
I just wanted to say Thank You
For the Golden box You left me
For the Wonder of who You are
That You gave this gift to me
Its meaning and its power
You must have known I needed
And I treasure every present
As they bless my life each day

WITHOUT MY GOD

I stumble as I rise to stand
My mouth would bite the feeding hand
My eyes don't look ahead for long
My mind would argue right to wrong
My ears would listen but fail to hear
The sound of reason though loud and clear
The only love that held me near
The only lives that found me dear
Are the ones God gave me
And I fear
That too will go away
Without my God

PASSING

A goodbye that waits

Lingering for a voice unheard

To call

For the Spirit in beginning and end

Without form

Yet recognizable

Draws to itself in its season

As a buzzard who tires of waiting

Approaches the kill and circles

No premise of salutations

No concern of details

No need

Of lengthy explanations

Personified it moves quickly

Patiently with purpose and function

And then when it is done

It flies away and is gone

Without the sting of death

THE WOUND

I see you

With my open mind

My open eyes

My open heart

I know the pain

That you felt

When you were wounded

I carried my wound

Over many experiences

And used it

Over and over

To justify

My hurting

I understand the numbness

The weariness of carrying weight

Too full

Too heavy

Too commanding

Too much

Relieved of the bondage

Of myself

I let the wound pass

Beyond where I stand

Around the universe and away

My smile will be the goodbye

As it moves on

And I am healed in my freedom

AND I CRIED

I said I would cry

He said it didn't matter

He didn't care

So I cried

And he left

When he came back

I was a little bit stronger

He said I will make you cry

And he did

So I cried

And he left

Not too long ago he returned

I had grown up

Older than when we first met

When I saw him

My legs strengthened underneath me

I stood taller

I looked at him

I saw him

He was old

Shriveled up

Bent over

Then he died

So I cried

And he was gone

TOO MANY TIMES

I can turn your negative comment
Into good
I can walk away
And forget
That your insult hurt
I can say
So that you can hear me
Ouch those words really stung
What I cannot do
Is look inside of you
And see your deepest motive
There could be so many reasons
That you choose to hurt others
Or chose to hurt me
Your need to feel something different
I can release my pain
And heal the wound
What I cannot do
What I will not do
Is stand in front of you
And let it happen again

FERTILE SOIL

From something that is built on sand
No solid life will grow
Such as the lessons seen today
The ones that come and go
To hold a light
A captured truth
And still have strength to stand
Is something planted deep inside
On pure and fertile land
So I break the ground within me
Casting rock and weed away
All nature's warmth replying
You will see new life today
The faith that there is planted
Will not wither will not die
But will lift its life light homeward
And reach up to the sky

PLAY TO WIN

I'm gonna buy me a ticket
To win a prize
I'm gonna play a game
Stand in the line
Behind and in front of others
I'm gonna get excited
And say that I have not won before
Then say
Well I won once
Then I'm gonna breathe
And get honest
With my self-knowing admit
That I have played and won
Many times
In different games
When I finally look up
After my self-correction
Even though I did not win this game
I am a Winner
If only because
I took the time
And bought the ticket

And stood in the line
And got honest
And played the game
And had fun
Which is after all
The best part of playing

TO CHOOSE AGAIN

A choice a choice

Not so still

This silent voice

Is calling for like kind to hear

Within their own self inner ear

A choice a choice

To choose again

This day to flow

Flowers bloom

Gently grow

That we will know

What we will know

That with choice

We choose

And then begin again

MEMORIES OF YOU

Out of one life comes another

Floating from creek, to river, to sea

Merrily laughing as time passes slowly

I see in your eyes

A reflection of me

PRECIOUS MEMORIES

In time we grow older

What dreams we remember

Joy brought at Christmas

Time spent together

Like the smile of a child

Or the face of a clown

The parade we all watched

As it lit up the town

This one thing in common

More precious than gold

The family we have

The love that we hold

Like the time spent in prayer

At the end of the day

The memories we have

That won't fade away

ABOUT THE POET

    Life has not broken Diane Everett's innocence. She acts on her belief that life is designed to be lived fully with passion and curiosity. Difficulties are opportunities to change course and find a better solution to whatever problem is perceived. Trials become road signs that if followed, can lead to a better perspective.

    Diane gets her creativeness through living, suffering, and surviving, thriving, always moving forward. Integrating grief in life offers wisdom, a beauty that leads beyond our daily lives, into a place where Spirit resides. Her creativity, her poems, come from that place.

    Inside her mind, her heart, she finds a common connection to other life forms. As she reaches out from her place of creative isolation, she brings an internalized and assimilated understanding of a common connection that we all share.

DISCUSSION GUIDE FOR BOOK CLUBS, JOURNALING, OR PERSONAL CONTEMPLATION

1. What in your life causes you to feel valued? What poems prompted you to consider your true value?
2. What poems brought you to reflect upon a higher understanding of your place in this world?
3. Which poem or poems promote an understanding of your own innocence?
4. How do you forgive? Which poems do you relate to when you consider forgiveness?
5. Which poem best inspires you to see the best in yourself and in your life?
6. How do you cope with daily difficulties? Which poem do you relate to about overcoming life's complexities?
7. Where does this poet's hope come from? Which poem best reflects that? Where does your hope come from?
8. In the challenges of the day where do you find your peace? Which poem inspires you to take a moment and be still?
9. What sets you free? In what poems is the author inspired to her own freedom? Which poem inspires you to be free?
10. What poems support the lifting of self-image to its highest perspective?

11. What poem reminds you of a time you were supported through love?
12. How do you express your love? What poem do you relate to that supports your way of giving love?
13. Which poem describes where the poet goes in a moment when it's too hard too tough, too much? Where do you go?
14. What life events have made you seek your own authentic self? What poem inspires you to continue to do that?
15. How do you support yourself to share your gifts? In what poem do you identify with a gift? How do you express your gifts?
16. At the beginning of the day, where do you get your strength? Which poem reminds you of where that that strength comes from?
17. In which poems did the poet express that she got stuck? What do you do to move past your limited ideas?
18. Which poems would lead you to believe in the healing power of unconditional love?
19. Which poem do you most identify with as your authentic self?
20. What poem best defines the internal determination not to let distorted emotions interfere with life? How do you manage your human emotions?
21. Which poem was most thought provoking for you and how did you relate to it?
22. In what way do you relate to the poet's willingness to change?

23. What poem inspires you to slow down, recenter and begin again?
24. What questions do these poems leave unanswered for you? What poem brought these questions forward?

About Sheltering Tree . Earth, LLC

We are an exclusive traditional publishing house, specializing in visionary and metaphysical fiction and nonfiction. Our readers, once they finish one of our books, will be able to get up and face the world wiser, stronger, centered, and with the assurance that we are not alone: we are all a part of the Sheltering Tree on Earth.

We encourage writers who would like more information about becoming one of our authors and poets to visit the website.

To set up interviews, speaking engagements, or book signing events with our authors and poets, please contact:

Evelyn Rainey, Publisher
ShelteringTree.Earth, LLC Publishing
PO Box 973 Eagle Lake, FL 33839
info@ShelteringTreeMedia.com
ShelteringTreeMedia.com

SHELTERING TREE

EARTH PUBLISHING

www.ingramcontent.com/pod-product-compliance
Lightning Source LLC
LaVergne TN
LVHW052101090426
835512LV00036B/3114